What Influenced You?

A Short Story Collection

Editor

SMITA VIVEK

Contents

Preface

This anthology is dedicated to all those noteworthy people and things making an impact or influencing us one way or the other. Influence, as we know, is that power which has the capacity to guide or even push us to make a change in the way we think, or act.

This influence can come from anywhere— from a movie we randomly decide to watch, or it can be a word we hear in a class that opens a whole new world, or it can come from a person older to us, or way too young, it can come from close friends or random strangers. Influence can come from anywhere— we just need to keep our hearts open to let it in, and settle deep within, so it can coax us to find our potential. Just as it happens in these collected stories.

The authors chosen for this anthology are all emerging short story writers. But they have all been through life and are still learning from it. In these past 6 months, we have taken inspiration from each other to work on making this collection possible. From them, I have learnt that there is no right age to learn something new, even if it is something about oneself. No one is too young or too old, we must just go ahead and do what is necessary, to make things work for us.

\- Smita Vivek
  Editor

Acknowledgments

I would like to thank my family for their support and for believing in me. A special thanks to my daughter, who is the force that pushes me to work harder each day.

I would like to extend my gratitude to all the contributors who trusted me with their stories and worked hard on making the improvements suggested during the process.

Finally, I would like to thank you for choosing to spend your time reading these stories. Hope you are inspired enough to contribute in my upcoming collection.

One

Young Tender Bloomers

Author Bio-Note

Mrs. Kamala Arunachalam is a retired Vice Principal of Royal College of Arts, Science and Commerce, Mira Road, Mumbai, India. Mrs. Kamala has been the Head of Mathematics Department and continues to serve as a Member of Management at the College.

She loves music, teaching, reading, writing, and exploring new places and cultures. She has consistently contributed to the college magazine PARWAZ, and has one article published in the Speaking Tree section of The Times of India.

Being a multi-talented person, Mrs. Kamala is known for many things, but she is cherished the most for being a kind and generous teacher. She has guided many students through their problems, be it mathematics or life.

"Hello madam," a voice from behind called out to me.

I had gone along with a friend on a Sunday evening for a stroll at Yellahanka Lake in the suburb of Bangalore.

This lake, which was on the verge of being extinct, was retrieved and restored to its old natural glory. Known for its bird population and bio diversity, it has been declared as bird conservation reserve. Mini islands abounding with trees and wild bushes are preserved for creating bird habitats, in keeping with their roosting and nesting activities. There is no direct access to these islands to ensure the aviation activities are undisturbed. Nevertheless, one can delightfully watch them from a distance.

That evening, we could spot some variety of storks, herons, and egrets. I could recognize a few, thanks to our college nature club for spreading awareness about the multicoloured amazing world of aerial sentient and educating us about their unique characteristics during their umpteen birding sessions.

I was enjoying a leisurely walk. The enchanting wild foliage under the clear blue sky, chirping of birds and the gentle breeze had a mesmerizing effect. Even so, for a fleeting moment my heart weighed heavy at depleting forest area, the ecological degradation all over the world and its disastrous consequences. But this patch of beauty made me wonder about the difference it would make to have such pockets of urban forests in every city.

With these thoughts I was strolling, when I heard this address. I turned to see a young woman pushing a pram with a baby sleeping in it. After a brief hesitation my heart skipped a beat. My eyes opened wide as I came face to face with Shiny, my student of computer science, after almost twelve years.

Generally, even if I may not recall their names, I surely do recognize my students instantly. Shiny was different, I remembered her well. Not only because she was an academically bright student, but also because she used to be very popular participating in lots of extracurricular events. She was conspicuous everywhere, always volunteering her services and organizing college festivals.

I vividly recalled, we had another student Sashi in the same batch, who was basically from Uttar Pradesh. She was a vernacular medium student in school. Though her fundamentals of the subjects were fairly good, she found it difficult to understand the lectures delivered in English, with all technical scientific terms. She was familiar with the Hindi translations but could not relate to the corresponding English terms. She was holding a poor mark sheet in the first-year groping in the terrain of uncertainty, almost deciding to quit studies. That is when Shiny stepped in. She offered herself to help Sashi with her problem.

Shiny used to spend hours with her, explaining the concepts in Hindi and helped her to clear all her arrears in the supplementary examination. From then on, they always sat together and Shiny continued diligently and dedicatedly to help Shashi with academics. She was a constant companion and transformed Sashi into a confident being by giving her complete moral support and encouragement. Needless to say, Sashi graduated with a reasonably good percentage.

Shiny had a knack to explain complex concepts in the simplest way unimaginable. During the intercollege academic festival, Shiny came up with a simple lighting arrangement to explain the complexity of linear transformation. I was awe struck with her creative brilliance! The following year she displayed a real snail as an example of Bezier curves found in nature. There were many such times when my students became my teachers. I had always been inspired by their zest, vigour, inquisitiveness, and innovative spirit.

I once needed to give a task to a student. I asked Shiny to suggest a few names. She came up with the right person, "Madam," she said, "Deepti may not be academically bright, but is very creative and sincere. She will do a good job." Shiny herself selected a small group of students to assist Deepti, and they all completed the task perfectly. As the MC of the event, Shiny complemented this group for their hard work and remembered to mention them while giving a vote of thanks. She was honest and genuinely cared for her fellow students.

Shiny was truly a born leader and a great speaker. I still remember bits of a very emotional speech Shiny gave during the college farewell, thanking everyone, from teachers to lab attendants. That was Shiny—an effective communicator and a charismatic person. She was extremely good at influencing her peers, a motivator, a budding leader, and a compassionate person.

College farewell parties happen only once in a student's life. The outgoing students are emotionally charged as they will be out of their comfort zone, a protected environment comprising their friends, teachers, and the lively college atmosphere, despite being aware of this inevitability. The students do come to their alma mater often in the initial stage after leaving, but these visits become fewer and far between once they start settling down in their careers and shouldering marital responsibilities. Our interactions dwindle, but we do try to make it a point to meet during annual alumni meet, but that too may not be possible for many for various reasons. But memories linger on, in fact remain everlasting.

Even though as teachers, we attend farewells every year, it feels sad to let go of these students with whom we interact for three years. Being a teacher, an emotional anchor, sharing their joys, sorrows, victories and loses, counselling them, and learning from them has always been rewarding. I confess being with the young enthusiastic students has been the most enjoyable part of my life.

Teaching, rather being a teacher has been beautiful and enriching.

So, this sudden and unexpected encounter with my student after so many years, transported me to my active teaching days. We hugged each other, sat on a bench, and started our conversation like long lasting friends. Instantly the time lapse melted, and the surroundings faded.

"My baby Advait, 5 months old," she said with explicit pride and bliss, "we stay close by.

How are you, madam? I think of you many times. After all, you encouraged me to be part of the organising team for our intercollege event, MATHSHOW. Only because of you I developed self-confidence to face the audience, without any stage fright," she ranted on happily.

"My dear Shiny, how can I forget you all? I have very fond memories of our times together. You all are an integral part of my life. Your madam has now retired, happily spending time travelling and reading to my hearts content."

"I am so happy to see you ma'am, sorry I have not been keeping in touch."

"That's ok dear. Tell me what are you doing now? in a lucrative corporate job? After all you were a bright computer science student, you did your post-graduation too if I remember correctly."

"Yes Madam, I completed my master's degree from Indian Institute of Science,

Bangalore and now I am teaching maths, science, and computer science in a government school."

I was flummoxed hearing this, "unbelievable" was my first reaction.

The reason for my surprise was one of my last conversations with her batch. Our third-year students are a very closely knit compatible group with whom we teachers interact very freely. We have lots of social debates and discussions. Once I asked all the students to speak about their dreams, desires, future plans. Everyone spoke about their careers. Almost all of them wanted to work in IT field, financial institutions, para medical lines, management courses, some had fairly good ideas about their own start up business, some even wanted to go ahead with research. I was no doubt happy that they had started thinking about a productive life but deep down I was disappointed that not a single student nourished a desire of becoming a teacher. As a brilliant student of computer science, Shiny obviously was very ambitious and was ready to plunge into a lucrative corporate world.

I voiced my disappointment, "Your parents want you all to go to good schools and colleges, to get the best of education, which means you had the best of teachers. From where will good, dedicated teachers come, if not from you all? How will your children tomorrow get good education?"

An immediate reply came from Shiny. "I love teaching, but you see there is no plush office, no high-power meetings in exotic locations, no exciting challenges, and not even an attractive pay cheque."

'Yes, indeed," I thought.

'Why not, these children are working hard and putting in their best efforts to be successful in academics. They deserve it.' My thoughts motioned.

"We also want to have a good house, a car, a posh life, and travel around the world.

What's wrong with that ma'am?"

"Well, of course, nothing wrong," I said.

My children were full of dreams. Somehow that moment did not seem appropriate to preach about leading a meaningful life, fulfilling one's obligation to the society et all.

Though the present generation has an excellent grasp and is highly informed, their material aspirations far outweigh their passion. Probably we as teachers have failed to curb their egocentric traits and instil a sense of social responsibility.

But here, my aggressive out-spoken student is telling me, "Ma'am, I have become a teacher not by default but by choice."

"I just did a brief stint as a teacher," she continued, "and as I was leaving for good, my students presented me with a bunch of flowers and an impromptu speech with tears in their eyes. I experienced a thrill, a warmth, a sense of satisfaction I never felt before.

That moment I realized where I belonged, to this vibrant youth who yearn to be understood and guided, whom I have the power to mould into a positive, productive force. A seemingly lacklustre vocation suddenly turned to be an exciting one. It was sort of a miraculous reincarnation. So, here I am a full-fledged teacher and am very happy for being one. Today, I realize what a wonderful fruitful life teachers like you have been leading— inspiring raw minds and ripening them to maturity."

I was stunned! This chit of a girl was giving me life lessons. It was overwhelming, a revelation to witness this student of mine reaching higher realms of morality. My heart swelled with pride!

I had tears of joy as I hugged her. It was a defining moment for me.

The sleeping baby woke up. "My child Advait. He is five months old." The joy and pride in her voice was evident. It was a sheer delight to see the baby giggling joyfully as I did a little baby talk with him.

"We come here quite often to enjoy the beauty and serenity, to soak in the fresh air listening to the music of birds, it is therapeutic. I also want to introduce the wonders of nature to my boy."

"Oh yes! It's never too early."

A pleasant young man, approached us with a smile, picked up the child in his arms. We had a mutual introduction session and an exchange of pleasantries.

"My husband has a startup company with a couple of partners. They are into making metallic polyethylene rod that is used to replace bones, in case of severe damage or if there is a need for replacement."

"Many established companies are already making it. But we did a lot of R and D with the metal alloy to make a lighter rod with lesser price, consequently reducing the expense of knee replacement and similar needs. We mostly supply to government hospitals, so that the benefit reaches the poor people," he elaborated.

"Ma'am. I remember our student charter with Einstein's words," Shiny interjected,

"A hundred times every day I remind myself that my inner and outer life depend on the labours of other men, living and dead, and that I must exert myself in order to give in the same measure as I have received and still receiving." She quoted verbatim.

"We will try to live up to it. Thank you, madam, for all the inspiration and encouragement given to me."

She bade farewell to me with a promise to keep in touch.

"And by the way, Sashi too is a teacher in an elementary school," she confided in me as a parting shot.

Wow, a double joy! Amazing! The value education imparted to them is not forgotten. It's actually being practiced. Our teachers' sincere efforts are paying off at the ground level.

I sat on the bench with an over whelming heart at this sudden unexpected and a rejuvenating experience. What can be more rewarding to a teacher than seeing her student passing the test of life with flying colours?

My own teachers appeared in my mind's eye. The teachers of yester years who worked for a meagre salary. But they believed that teaching was a noble profession, taught us even outside classrooms, imparted life lessons and contributed to our character building. They have discretely passed on the qualities of a good teacher by being an example themselves. I gratefully remembered them and thanked them from my heart.

A teacher should possess an art to instil a state of mind in young pupils who are full of wonder and thirst to learn, and also the craft to go over to their level, take them by the hand and guide them to recognize and realize their potential. A teacher is an ordinary soul with an extraordinary commitment. One is lucky if one could find this figure to be very benevolent and life transforming.

These dynamic, sensitive, enlightened, young tender bloomers like Shiny equipped with the art and craft of teaching, have immense calibre to transform the life of their pupils. The chain will continue.

My life has not been wasted. As I sat in the quietude of the serene surroundings, an absolute peace engulfed me. Suddenly I noticed that the colour of the sky was a brilliant crimson red. Nature seemed to be in a festive mood, celebrating the triumph of goodness and piety.

Two

The Greatest Influence

Author Bio-Note

Mrs Kanchan Agrawal is a successful academician, poet, YouTuber, and a critic. She has been imparting knowledge to students of various grades for last 20 years.

Apart from her articles, poems and reports being published in school and college magazines, she has also reviewed some of the English Grammar and Biology books.

She got the first recognition for her work when she composed her first poem in English to participate in the AIFEST Poetry Competition-2023 on International Women's Day. Her poem was selected in A-grade category and found a place in their anthology 'Embracing the Feminine.'

She loves to pen down her emotions, feelings, and frustrations in the form of poems and articles. She intently believes in the proverb 'Books are our best friends' that helps you relieve stress. Hope she finds a good place in many more such books as this one.

"Now we present the most awaited award 'The Best Student of the Year'." Suddenly someone comes and whispers something into the anchor's ears.

"Hey Guys! There's a surprise for you all – a special prize for a very special student. And that very special student is none other than Miss Kanchan Agrawal. She is being awarded for her relentless hard work and dedication, especially in Maths."

"May I request Mrs Roshni Kelkar to ascend the dais to give away the award and say a few words."

There was applause all around. As I stood up to receive the award, tears embraced my cheeks. It was like a glamorous moment for me – the flashlights flooding me and the spot light tracing my footsteps walking up to the stage. All eyes were on me but my eyes only waited for a glimpse of Mrs. Kelkar on the stage.

Receiving an award from my favourite and beloved teacher like Mrs Kelkar was a proud moment for me. I still remember the day. It was 17th of October 1992 - our Annual Day. All the awardees were waiting for their turn to come. I took my seat in the audience waiting to watch different performances and to clap for those being awarded. But the announcement of this special award to my name made me go dumbstruck.

I did receive awards before in school but those were for the achievements I knew about. But this was rather a shock than a surprise to me, a shock that brought cheers in my life. Who knew such a day would come when I, Kanchan Agrawal, would finally get recognition for all my hard work. That day stands as clear as yesterday for me, because nothing as special as this had ever happened before. That day was truly a turning point.

"Dear students," the words interrupted my chain of thoughts. "We come across number of students in our life. They all have different calibres in them. But the potential, the acme, the rigor that I found in Miss Kanchan was incredible. She is passionate and always tried to put her best foot forward. She never hesitated in biting the bullet and putting her nose to the grindstone. The zeal that I saw in her is rarely found. All these qualities made us decide and announce this special award. Her relentless hard work has borne fruits today."

Today even after 30 years, these words remain afresh in my mind. They still motivate me whenever I am down.

I still remember the day when I entered Class 11th. I was a shy and timid girl. It was 7th of July 1990 when I first saw Mrs Kelkar in my Maths class. She was a tall, slim, and middle-aged lady clad in a lemon-yellow sari and no make-up at all. Though 50-55 years old, the smile on her face made her look younger and even more attractive. As she entered the class, she greeted everyone with a smile. The class progressed and I realised she was not only simple and sober in appearance but also firm and disciplined when it came to studies. I was totally moved by her simplicity. Even in her firmness, she managed to be kind.

She was a very hard working and patient woman, always ready to help others and that was what I liked about her. She knew each student by name. Her memory was so sharp that she even remembered which child had what problem and in which sum. She was never rude to students. Whosoever approached her, she dealt with them very kindly. It was this nature that exhorted me to approach her with my problems.

It all started when I took admission in Class 11th and opted Science. Till then I was good at all my subjects. But the moment I came across Maths in class 11th, the first shock that I received was my inability to comprehend Maths.

Till Class 10th I studied only Algebra and Geometry as my Maths subjects but Class 11th and 12th Maths was totally a different ball game. Except Algebra and Geometry, it had all the different types of topics like limit, parabola, hyperbola, matrices, permutation, combination, trigonometry, function and what not. All these topics were beyond my understanding. Despite all my efforts, I failed to understand these heavy concepts and hence was unable to solve any of the problems. The result was, for the first time in my life, I failed in Maths. In fact, it was the first time I failed at anything. Nothing broke my heart as that mark-sheet with a bold capital 'F' in red ink.

Those days, neither tuitions or coaching were so common, nor my family was financially strong enough to send me to coaching. I had to manage it all myself. It was then that Kelkar Madam came forward and agreed to help and support me at every step. Now, I was found spending all my free time with my Maths Teacher, solving the same questions number of times.

YES, 'SAME QUESTIONS' number of times. But salute to her patience! Neither did she ever refuse to solve my doubts nor I ever found her frustrated. I don't know how and when I imbibed that quality in me and now as a teacher myself, I too am able to handle my students and guide them with the same patience.

But the journey hadn't been so easy. Approaching Kelkar Madam for all small doubts every time made me a prey for bullies.

Students started teasing and calling me 'Bookworm,' 'Miss Genius,' 'Teacher ki Chamchi', 'Padhaku,' and what not. And at that age, I was sensitive to such comments and it brought down my morale. So, I stopped going to her. As I said earlier, she remembered each child by his/her name and problems. Maybe she understood my problems, both in Maths and beyond maths as well.

One day she called me and asked, "Kanchan, are you able to solve sums now?"

I timidly replied, "Yes Ma'am."

She read my face. She immediately understood that I was lying.

She said, "Would you mind doing some sums here?"

I hesitantly nodded, knowing fully well how this was going to go. She gave me a simple sum and asked to solve it in front of her. And as she correctly read my face, I could not solve it. I started crying. At this, she put her hands on my shoulder and consoled saying,

"See Kanchan, if you are not going to get your problems solved, the problems are only going to increase further. Why are you not coming to me now-a-days with your doubts?"

"I am sorry, Ma'am. I really feel embarrassed to come to you with the same problem again and again," I admitted.

With a warm expression she said, "Dear, there is no need to feel ashamed or embarrassed to come and get your doubts solved. We are here to help students in all the possible ways. I understand all students cannot understand all the subjects or have equal interest in them."

After a short pause she continued, "Ok, tell me one thing why did you pursue Science and what is your favourite subject?"

"Biology," I replied with great excitement, "Because I want to know who I am and what I am. I also want to know the deep secrets lying in nature."

"Now see, Maths and Biology are opposite subjects. Where Maths is a technical subject, Biology needs lots of learning. The practical aspects of both the subjects are very different from each other. If I am asked to study Biology, maybe, I would also face the same problem that you face in Maths. So, there is no need to be scared about anything. Do come to me whenever you feel so, or you are unable to solve any problems. With problems I do not mean only Maths related problems, I also mean your personal problems. So, come on now, give me a smile."

We both laughed whole heartedly. I felt quite relieved. Those kind words soothed my bereaved heart. Thereafter, I started spending a lot of time with her trying to understand not just Maths, but also small-little life lessons.

Here, I would like to take a detour and tell you something else about my life. I come from a conservative and orthodox family, a family where girls have no freedom.

Convincing my family to let me continue my studies after 10th was a struggle on its own. In addition to that, there were numerous instances where my education almost came to an end. I accepted all the challenges and had to make a lot of sacrifices. There were times when it was too difficult for me to move forward. In such times, it was again Kelkar Madam, who as Godmother came to help me. She taught me how to stay focussed on my goal. It was really because of her that I started enjoying my classes, and stayed motivated to pursue my studies against all odds.

It is truly said **'TEACHERS' ARE SECOND MOTHERS'**. They have a great impact on a child's life. It is often found that a child starts to believe more in their teachers, even more than their parents. Children admire their teachers so much that they even start imitating them unconsciously. Most probably every child in their childhood wishes at least once to be a teacher as a grown-up. Such is the impact of a teacher.

Anyways, time kept flying, I kept struggling. I hardly spent any time on other subjects apart from completing the required work. I lost my hunger and sleep. Maths became a nightmare. I was engrossed in my Maths work so much that even in dreams I kept on solving Maths problems (or as told by my mother). Even during the examination days, I spent only two hours on other subjects and the remaining time was utilised in solving Maths.

Then came the result day. It was 26th of April 1991. I still remember how nervous I was that day. There was no excitement of the result on my face at all. As the roll numbers were called out, my heart kept throbbing and when it was my turn, my heart beat was at its peak. The first thing I wanted to see in my result was my score in Maths. I was like a cat on hot bricks. Everything went blur. Despite all efforts none of the marks were clear to my eyes.

I tried to calm my nerves down and finally what I saw made me very emotional. I *managed to pass with just passing marks.* Many of us may not understand the importance of those passing marks but for me it was like I was on cloud nine.

When I went to thank my Maths Teacher for her support, I came to know about another surprising news- that I scored the highest in Chemistry. It was almost unbelievable for me because I hardly devoted anytime for any other subjects other than Maths. This result not only boosted up my morale but I also developed a sense of confidence.

That day, overwhelmed with the result, I cried inconsolably. Mrs. Kelkar consoled me saying my success was the result of my perseverance. This is the greatness of any teacher – giving all the credit to the child. That day became one of the most cherished days of my life. Every teacher in the department congratulated me for my achievement. Though small, it was a much-awaited achievement for me.

Now, I was in class 12th. Syllabus was much tougher and I was seriously obsessed with Maths by now. But my Maths Teacher, Mrs Kelkar *never let me down*. Because of my teachers' continuous efforts, I started relishing my studies. But getting marks in Maths was still a tedious task for me. My obsession over-powered me and I started seeing Maths everywhere. While making rotis and chapatis, I started calculating parabola and hyperbola according to its shape and size. Not only these, utensils, television, fans all turned into different dimensions and had to be evaluated.

Instead of being happy about my efforts, my mother was terribly worried about my episodes, as she called them. She thought it would be better for me if I stopped studying and focussed on what girls are actually supposed to focus on. It took a lot of explaining and begging to convince and make her realise what my actual problem was. I also told her about the help and support I was receiving from my Maths Teacher and other teachers. Finally, she agreed. Half the problem was solved but main problem i.e. getting marks in Maths remained the same.

The struggle continued (actually, it was my Maths teacher's struggle too) and finally I passed my 12th Board with flying colours. The biggest feather in my cap was my marks in Maths. I scored 68/100 which was really a big achievement for me. Today, I am 50 years old, but the days I spent on Maths are still as fresh in my mind. These memories do not allow me to be lethargic at any point of time.

Thereafter, I continued studying and completed my graduation. There too I found many teachers supporting me all the time.

During my graduation, the entire syllabus of Classes 11th and 12th changed. Since the teachers were not able to receive any training by then, I was often called to help and carry out the Biology practical for my junior college. I found it as a good opportunity to express my gratitude to them. But after marriage, things changed. I was able to meet them only once and I still bear this grudge in my heart. I know many of them would not be alive today but they all are alive in my heart in the form of a teacher – a profession that I took up because of their sacrifice, commitment, and help extended towards me.

The seed of dedication that was sown that time still bears the fruit. I wasn't able to complete my Masters, rather I would say, I was not allowed to. According to my mother, I was the first girl child in the entire family, including the relatives, to have completed my graduation. Now, she was not at all in favour of allowing me to continue my studies. She always wanted to see me married and taking care of my family, just as she did. I think that was one of the reasons apart from social pressure because of which she wanted me to discontinue my higher studies.

Even after marriage, I did not get the chance to pursue my studies. But I kept struggling. With great struggle I managed to get a B. Ed. and PGDCA degrees. The struggle continued for 27 long years.

Then came the year 2020. The entire world was in the clutches of Corona when I came to know about a 'Master's Degree in Food and Nutrition' which can be pursued online. I found a good opportunity to fulfil my dream being at home and taking care of my family members. I enrolled myself in the course and completed it in the year 2022. Now, finally at the age of 50, my Master's degree is in my hand. I am thankful to Corona, which came into my life as a blessing in disguise and gave me a wonderful chance to achieve my goal. I know it was a difficult time for most of the population, and I mean no disrespect to anyone who suffered during the time. But for me, the two years came with an opportunity I was longing to get for years. Here again, I would like to give, some if not all, the credit to Kelkar Madam whose encouraging words did not let the spark to continue my studies die out. Thank you, Kelkar Madam! If you hadn't been with me in my heart and soul motivating me all the time, I wouldn't have been able to achieve this success.

Today as a teacher, I can vouch for the satisfaction of watching children reach their potential, the joy of helping someone in achieving something. As a teacher, I too came across many such students who really needed help and I tried my level best to guide them in all the possible ways, whether it is motivational guidance, working on their academics, or any other grounds.

Post-covid, two amazing things happened which made me feel loved and appreciated. One of them was the big tussle from students who wanted to study English only from Kanchan Ma'am and nobody else. Though my education was in the field of Science, as a teacher I am better known as an English teacher. The fight meant I was doing something right, and that my years of dedicated work have not gone unnoticed.

And the other one came as a phone call- one day, as I reached home, I got a call from an unknown number. By the time I could settle my bags, I missed the call. Only then did I notice the number of missed calls from the same number. As I wondered who it was, I got the call again. Worried that it could be a bad news, I received the call anxiously, but the voice on the other side sounded quite exciting. "Good Afternoon, Ma'am," a male voice greeted.

"Good Afternoon Sir", I replied.

"Madam, we have heard a lot about you and wish to offer you the post of 'Vice Principal' in our school. Would you like to join us?"

I could not believe my ears. I was stunned.

"Hello, hello, Ma'am!" I regained my senses and "Yes Sir, I surely would love to" replied assertively. "Could you please tell me more about your school and the responsibilities please?" I continued.

The meeting lasted for almost two hours. Finally came- "Congratulation Ma'am! We are glad to welcome you to our family as 'The Vice Principal' of our school."

The world had been very different that day, an another turning point in my life. Today, 11th of December 2023, I stepped in the school as 'The Vice Principal.' Everything had been different for me now. The world was a changed place. I was officially introduced as 'The Vice Principal' in the School Assembly. My opening speech enthralled the audience. Another glamorous moment, as on stage I could see students, teachers, even Directors applauding and giving their best wishes.

As once I waited to see Kelkar Madam on the stage, today I stood at the same place as a renowned personality. I wish and pray that she watches me today from the audience. I am sure she would be proud to see me reach this position. Her student, who shied away from clarifying her Maths doubts because of some bullies, was standing on the stage, giving a speech as a Vice Principal. Oh, what a blessing!

Finally, I was taken to 'MY CABIN' (yes, my personal cabin) and handed over the charge formally. The day, though very hectic, had been very inspiring, motivating, and full of fun and frolic. The entire scenario was a changed one now.

It is sad to know that this noble profession is becoming a business for many now-a-days. I realised this as I hold this position and see things as an administrator.

Some teachers work only for money and not the joy of giving. There are very few students who are as dedicated and devoted as they used to be. There were days when students obeyed, respected, and worshipped their teachers but now students need full freedom, good marks, and pass out without struggle. The way the rules are changing, teachers' hands are bound, students are taking the advantage of this and ruining their own lives. Despite all facilities, students are not making the best use of their teachers.

Fortunately, there are still some dedicated teachers who have maintained the glory of the profession and earned a unique place in students' lives. But the orthodox thinking of the society has not changed much. In my career of 18 years, I still find several

'Kanchan's' in the society. To cite an example, once I came across one such Kanchan who faced the same environment and struggled to understand and learn English. It took three long years for her to cope up with the subject. As a teacher, I tried my level best to be like Kelkar Madam and share the love I received from my teachers, to my students.

It's true that every teacher cannot be a Dronacharya and every student an Eklavya. I don't know whether I am an Eklavya or not but Mrs. Kelkar was definitely a Dronacharya for me who taught me, like an Eklavya, how to be dedicated; like an Arjun, how to target an eye (my goal); like a Bhim, fight all odds (struggles of life); and like a Yudhishthir, to be firm and stand for the right.

In our Indian culture, a teacher occupies a place superior to God. A teacher is considered to possess the powers of Lord Brahma who identifies the inborn talents and polish the skills, Lord Vishnu who trains and guides a student to the right path and Lord Shiva who helps fight all evils and destroy it.

This example reminds me of a *Doha* of Sant Kabir Das Ji:

"गुरु गोविंद दोऊ खड़े,

काके लागू पाय।

बलिहारी गुरु आपने,

गोविंद दियो बताए।।"

Kelkar Madam, you have always been a source of inspiration for me and will always occupy a sacred place in my heart.

Three

The First Rule of
The Fight Club
Is...

Author Bio-Note

Mr. Parthsarathi Dikonda is a very enthusiastic, creative, and multitasking artist. A quintessential ambivert, who takes up writing as a source of expression and escape. He first started writing in his post graduate years when he had dilemmas about his choice of career and future.

He wrote poems and articles for college magazines and this recognition pushed him to write more. He also wrote for various websites, and won online literary competitions.

He is a big movie buff which influences his style of writing and content, too. He loves to write movie reviews, for which he also won prizes.

This short piece has autobiographical tone to it, as it talks about how that one movie inspired me to finally make a decision as I stood on the crossroad.

"Its only after we have lost everything that we are free to do anything"

Apologies to everyone who has witnessed 'Fight Club' as I am going to break the first and second rule of fight club by talking about it. Being a cinephile, my life is influenced by movies in many intervals. And Fight Club stays right on the top.

I was a studious kid since childhood, doing well in academics, trying to prove myself to my parents by scoring well in school. My mother was a teacher in the same school that I was studying, so I was always under surveillance and under pressure of being a quintessential good student. With a little focus on studies, I made it into the merit list of the board exams, after which I was given a choice to select among different fields according to my liking. But as a decent scoring individual in a brown household, you never really have a choice except choosing the field of science. So that is what I did.

But after ten years of constant burden of proving myself, I thought of blowing off some steam and relaxing for those two years, neglecting the academics and that obviously affected my results in the higher secondary examination and I could barely qualify for first class grading.

My parents realized that keeping me in my comfort zone would jeopardize my academics, so they decided to admit me into a different university, away from home, in a new place, amidst new people. Prior to that, I also interned for a month in my uncle's company. This actually did help in my academics, as being an introvert; I didn't bother making a lot of new friends in that new place. I would attend lectures regularly, study for rest of the time, rebuilt my reputation as a smart and studious student. On the other hand, I was among the top five scorers of my Post-Graduate degree. Thus, creating a dilemma in choosing the correct field for my future.

"Advertising has us chasing cars and clothes, working jobs we hate so that we can buy thing we don't need"

I came back home with the result which made my parents' eyes' sparkle. They were determined that I was made for the academics, therefore, encouraging me to take up a job. I started going for interviews unwillingly. I cracked an interview and received a 9-5 job in a Food testing lab as a Quality Analyst. The work was interesting at the beginning as it was application oriented, I liked the process but it got repetitive and stagnant after a while. That was my boring life, typical routine, perpetual loop of mundane mediocrity. No one would want to watch such a movie, right? But there is a parallel story, so let's rewind my story a little.

Along with academics, I excelled in extracurricular activities, too. Prominently, as a dancer. Dancing gave me immense joy. I would participate in all the cultural functions throughout school and college. As soon as my college life started, I made the 'room for cultural activities' my second home. Bunking lectures and spending the whole year in that room, meeting new people, learning other art forms along with dance, participating in university competitions, winning, celebrating, and living my life to the fullest. Even when I was away from home in a new place, I found myself performing on stage for annual functions, and winning over a completely new set of audience, becoming "that famous guy" of the college. I felt this passionate ecstasy and I knew that this is exactly what I want in my life— stage, lights, loud music, and the sweet sound of audience applauding. But I had no proper direction.

"We have all been raised on television to believe that one day we'd all be millionaires, and movie gods and rock stars; but we won't. And we are slowly learning that fact. And we are very, very pissed off"

But I was conditioned in a way that taking up creative field as a career was never on my radar. Both my parents were simple office goers with secure and stable income and they wanted the same for me. People around me would also say that it's a gamble to bet on such a volatile sector and quote ideas like 'a known devil is better than an unknown angel.'

Everyone was being so sceptical that it scared me from going against them. At that point in life, going against everyone and failing would mean lifelong regret and disappointment. There would always be the fear of failure lurking at the back of my neck. As I had no firm support, I couldn't dare to take a stand for myself, and continued the job.

Just when I thought I would have a boring climax, there came a twist, with upbeat music in the background, like a cameo entry, stood in front of me- 'Fight club'. A cult movie for movie lovers, this movie claims to have changed lives of many people, and I can testify to that. With influencing dialogues and philosophical monologues, this movie preaches the way of living.

The scene that influenced me the most is when the protagonist takes a convenient store owner, Raymond, as a hostage, and asks him on point blank, "what did you want to become in life?" Raymond says that he wanted to be a veterinarian but because he lacked money and due to other familial responsibilities, he had to quit studying and work at a store for money. The protagonist,

Tyler Durden, asks Raymond that would he die here, on his knees, in the backyard of his store, or would he rather live his dream. Tyler takes Raymond's license from his wallet and threatens him saying he should be on his way for veterinarian study in 6 weeks, or Tyler will find him and kill him. And he sets him free.

Upon being asked why he did this, Tyler says that tomorrow will be the most beautiful day of Raymond's life; his breakfast will taste better than any meal that you and I have tasted.

This scene pierced my conscience on a spiritual level. Like finding the purpose of life. Should we die, doing the job that we hate just because the society expects us to, or should we rather chase our dream, our passion, and live the life on our terms. It gave me the courage to turn my life upside down and steer it on a completely different track.

"Hitting bottom is a weekend retreat, its not a god damn seminar. Stop trying to control everything and just let go"

Being a night owl, I never liked waking up early. So I started finding excuses to take a leave from work. But dancing was that one thing for which I would be excited to open my eyes at the earliest of hours and get out of the bed. This was my sign from the universe. To let go off control, to focus more on the work I love. And this proved to be the last nail in the coffin. They were clearly the signs from the universe to tell me what my body is meant to be doing. The global phenomenon that came as a curse for millions of people came as a blessing for me.

The lockdown due to the Corona Pandemic paved my way towards quitting my job. My parents also realized that no job is as secured as they would like to believe. There were many people they knew personally losing their so-called permanent jobs. And also, that death is so unpredictable, why waste it in on doing things that we don't want to.

Like a Special appearance in a movie, my brother-in-law came for the rescue and gave me that support and push that I always needed. He trusted me and believed in my talent, he convinced my parents, and helped me plan and organize the steps to make the future of my dreams. That is how I could gather courage in building my own dance studio. Step by step I started exploring the field, expanding the scope, learning, teaching, and so on.

Things were not as expected. Earlier, when I danced just for fun, there were not many restrictions, not even judgements. No milestones or benchmarks to be set or achieved. People would look at it just as an X-factor and applaud for my passion. But when I took dancing professionally, the attitude changed. I faced a lot of criticism for smallest of my mistakes. Sometimes, I wondered if my decision to choose dancing as a career was wrong. But I kept brushing such thoughts aside and tried to excel in what I do. So, I learnt through practice, a lot of practice. I improvised and kept experimenting with different forms and combination.

"*You are not your job, you are not the money in your bank, you are not the content of your wallet, you are the all singing all dancing crap of the world*"

This was my roller coaster ride from being a confused nerd to a super cool entrepreneur. Now I own a dance studio, I teach dance in schools and run classes, I also choreograph for different events like weddings. I even perform at prestigious programs. And most importantly, I am happy with the life that I have chosen. The only thing that kept me motivated through my journey was that I won't have any regrets, of not trying, of not giving myself enough of what I love. If this goes downhill, I won't have anyone to blame, not even myself, because I gave my best. I stopped worrying about my decision. I decided to spread my arms and be the all singing, all dancing crap of the world.

What Influenced You?

Four

Rejuvenating Empathy

Author Bio-Note

Ms. Praghya is a student of Holy Cross College, Trichy, pursuing her Bachelor's degree in English Literature. She is an idealist, empath and groundbreaker who strives to make a difference in the world. She aspires to be a source of inspiration and to live a virtuous life. Her areas of interest are psychology, music, and poetry. She has published an E-book of an anthology "Mesmerizing Nature" through True Dreamster Press. She walks one with the modern world and also upholds her culture and traditions. She also actively takes part in various competitions on poems, short stories, and flash fiction on both at national and international level.

Ms. Jayapriya Durga is an Assistant Professor in the PG and Research Department of English, Holy Cross College, Trichy. She has ten years of teaching experience and passionate about instilling ethical values among the student community.

Her areas of interest are Postcolonial Studies, Literary Criticism, English Language Teaching and Creative writing. She is currently pursuing her Ph.D on Postcolonial Literature and Cultural studies. She has published a collection of poems titled Discover your Learning at LangLit: An International Peer Reviewed Open Access Journal, UGC Approved Journal- Arts and Humanities in Vol.4Issue:1. As a techno savvy educator she motivates her students to use digital tools effectively by assigning innovate tasks. In addition to her teaching responsibilities, she actively participates in both national and international conferences and seminars, where she presents papers on her research and engages with fellow scholars.

In a bustling city, called Myrandur, located in the ever hot, central southeastern region of the country's borders, lived an idiosyncratic girl. She resided in a rustic apartment with her parents and her younger sister. Her parents, even in this modern era, are still bound to their age-old customs and are narrow minded. They have strong opinions about how they want the people in the house to be and act. However, from the very beginning, this young girl has been breaking away from their mindset and trying to find her true self.

"Ahana, we have a function tonight. Get ready on time," marched Maha into Ahana's room. Gazing intently at the young girl lying on her bed, immersed in her book.

I'd rather be home alone, Mom. "I've a lot of work to be done, Mom. I can't make it, you guys have a good time," Ahana looked at her mom with a slight hope that she would understand Ahana's dislike towards crowded places at least this time.

Maha stared at her for a minute that felt longer, huffed, and slammed the door shut as she rambled on about how disrespectful kids are these days.

Ahana let out a long sigh. *Those who live for the society, neglect their own loved ones' needs.* Her eyes stinging, she looked at a picture of two strangers in her book. A woman carrying a child in her arms, looking at each other, their eyes crinkled in joy and pupils dilated in love. And here, in the real world, it was always just doubt and disappointment in her mother's eyes. *A loving Mom…,* her voice came out as a whisper as she caressed the lady's face as if real. An empty void filled her chest with longing.

Can I ever be loved? As much as Ahana wanted an answer for it, she knew this wasn't the time to dwell into complex matters. She went through her to-do-list, placing them to priority and set to work.

Ahana is a young girl in her twenties with an intrapersonal nature. Just as she could reflect on her true feelings, she could also read other people and believed that, *"Every individual has an untold story."*

While some saw faces, I saw stories—stories in the form of silent narratives etched in the subtle gestures and fleeting expressions of those I encountered. My journey into the world of understanding people began in childhood, as I unravelled the intricate threads of conversation and behaviour that wove the tapestry of my life.

While others played with toys, I was engrossed in a different game altogether. I observed the people around me with an intensity that bordered on fascination. Their behaviour, their actions, their words – it was as if each gesture and utterance held a cryptic code I was destined to decipher.

One night as she worked on her project, she heard a soft knock on her door. Her friend Shalini entered the room with a big hopeful smile. Peeping in playfully, giggling and waved at worn-out Ahana excitedly. Ahana swallowed the lump in her throat, stopping the tears forming in her eyes, which didn't go unnoticed by Shalini. "Hey! I've been trying to reach you for ages! What's keeping you so busy young lady?" piped in Shalini as she hugged a tired looking Ahana. Her small body slightly warm which raised Shalini's concern.

"Ugh long day..." Ahana started, but she noticed the restlessness in Shalini's eyes. So instead of talking about her troubles, she enquired about Shalini. "What happened? Are you alright?"

She let out a long sigh and sat across Ahana, expressing her distress about her family issues while Ahana looked at her with worry and held her hands caressing them. "They don't understand how stressful college life is, Ahana. I try helping around the house as much as I can but I need to finish my projects and I need rest! I'm a human who gets tired, aren't I?"

Ahana listened to everything without interrupting, nodding and humming as she spoke. In the end, she tried comforting her, "They had a tough life sweetheart. All they want is to make their kids stronger for the future. I agree, their methods are pretty harsh and seem inconsiderate sometimes. But that's 'cause they have been taught that way and are unaware of the various other impacts it would have on the kids. Tell them, talk to them, and express your emotions. Parents who love you would always want the best for you."

Ahana caressed her hair and spoke in a gentle voice, assuring her it's gonna be okay.

Shalini visibly relaxed a little and gave a small smile as she nodded at Ahana in understanding.

They continued to talk and joke around for some more, when Shalini asked her what she was doing. "The creative writing project! I've been working on pending work for hours and it just doesn't end!" sighed Ahana.

"Oh yeah, it was an open topic, right? What did you choose?" asked an excited Shalini.

"Oh um... it's... about psychology and how it helped me battle through low self-esteem and loneliness... uhh... I-It's stupid, right? I-I..."

"It's incredible."

Ahana looked at Shalini with wide eyes, completely speechless.

"That's such an out-of-the-box idea! I never thought someone majoring in English could write about Psychology. How do you get such amazing ideas?"

Before she could say more, Shalini noticed a drop of tear rolling down Ahana's cheeks. Worried, Shalini held Ahana's shoulders, as she broke down.

Shalini knew what was going on. She had been trying to make space for Ahana to process her emotions and get comfortable enough to let it out. She was relieved it happened before she could leave, "There, there. It's okay. Let it all out... I got you."

Shalini let Ahana have her moment, hugging her tightly and caressing her back, as minutes passed by. Her tears straining Shalini's clothes as her sobs echoed in her room. Slowly, Ahana started calming down, "Here, drink some water. You don't have to act tough in front of me. I'll always stand by your side, no matter what. We've been friends for long enough for me to know what's in your heart," nodding Ahana leaned into her as she patted Ahana's head while smiling.

Ahana was good at understanding other's feelings because she spent, what felt like her life time, regulating her own feelings when things would go wrong in her life. Yet possessing the ability to regulate one's emotions doesn't make them completely self-sufficient. Ahana longed for recognition and appreciation. And once in a while, a kind word was enough to break through everything she was holding in tight.

Shalini understood Ahana's nature very well. "Silly girl, you're always there for others yet you never word out your worries." Shalini playfully hit Ahana's shoulder, as Ahana tried hiding her face in her embrace. "I know it's really hard to be a part of such a difficult family. Not many would understand as it's uncommon and unheard of. It baffles me that your Dad is so robotic in nature and your Mom...," she sighs "A parent shouldn't project their insecurities on their kids... I'm here for you. I might not be a mind expert like you but I can still comfort you to my best."

Ahana nodded, hugging Shalini tighter, taking in the warmth she had been longing for. "How much did you complete? Will you be able to finish the project today? The submission is tomorrow." Shalini questioned Ahana as she caressed her hair and arms.

"I might have to pull an all-nighter if it's not done by dinner," sniffed Ahana.

"You always manage to pull it through even if it's last minute. Maybe try working on things sooner? It could be easy on you too, Ms. Perfectionist," suggested Shalini. Ahana nodded, smiling. It eased her mind to know that someone cares for her.

It's funny how despite trying our best to be emotionally independent, other's opinion always has an impact. Be it positive or negative. For Ahana, it was a little stronger.

Maybe it stemmed from her mother, Maha, who was always conscious about 'what others would think or say.' Maha's intense nature of wanting everything to be picture perfect made her self-conscious and controlling. Maybe her intensions are not to hurt others, but she ends up hurting everyone, especially Ahana. From what clothes to wear, to how to keep her hair, to how to sit and stand, sometimes even breathing. "You're breathing too fast Ahana, that's not how you are supposed to breathe," she would say.

Maha wanted Ahana to be perfect in every way. But she failed to realise the negative effects of such controlling behaviour. Maha thought it was love. But all Ahana could feel was the lack of space to be herself. Ahana felt anxious around Maha, and longed to be accepted by her mother for who she was. Ahana fell into depression and questioned her individuality for years. Her self-esteem kept deteriorating and she deemed herself unlovable and believed that love is conditional. Her anxiety was triggered at the most causal comments or situations.

The solution came to her during one of the Psychology lectures at college. Ahana was learning about emotions and the power of regulating them. She was curious to know more. She turned to the library and her teachers. This saved her. She acted on what her gut was telling her. Her readings and the guidance from her teachers made her realise that she cannot change her mother or any situation she faces. She needs to work on herself. She then practised relentlessly on regulating her emotions. Maha's constant battering, which once pushed Ahana into depression, turned into an opportunity to put into practice whatever Ahana learnt.

We look for love and recognition outside the house, when we don't get enough of it from home. Ahana has thus, resorted to look for validation from her friends and strangers, because she had given up hope for recognition from home.

Ahana was not always alone though. She had her grandmother, Gayathri. Her biggest source of joy growing up. Her grandmother saw her potential right from the beginning. She would tell Ahana stories of how even as a toddler, she would keenly observe how people eat, talk, walk, and would imitate them.

As a child, Ahana was always a people's person. And with time, even though Ahana started closing herself to others, she enjoyed her time with her grandma, or Maa as she called her. Maa would tell Ahana bedtime stories and hold her snug till she fell asleep. She would cheer for her for the tiniest achievements and yet be firm with her when Ahana needed to be disciplined.

As Ahana grew up, Maa shielded her from difficult family members. Once as a pre-teen, the family was invited to a relative's place for some function. Maha scolded Ahana for choosing to wear a pair of pants and a cute kurti. Maha commented on how the pants made her thighs look too fat and the colour of the kurti made Ahana look too dark.

Believing each word, Ahana assumed she looked horrible and refused to go for the function. After a lot of coxing, Ahana opened up to Maa about Maha's comments. Gayathri could not believe her daughter-in-law would make her grandchild feel this way. Gayathri chided Maha about the situation.

This and a whole lot of other incidents, however, turned out to be the reason why Maha sent her mother-in-law away from Ahana. Somehow, Ahana's grandparents moved to another city, up the northern part of country, to live with their eldest son and his family. Maha did not like being scolded in front of her daughter and being told that she was wrong.

This was a blow to Ahana, who lost her support and her chance at feeling loved at home. Ahana built walls around her and replied in nods and very few words after that, for many years. She missed Maa every day. She lost the person she talked about her day at school, she missed the person who taught her how to eat a mango in a fun manner.

Most of her teen years were spent in believing that her hair was too curly, her skin-tone too uneven, her legs too fat and arms too thin, etc.

The presence of a younger sister made things a little better as Ahana focused on giving Mishti the love she did not receive.

Loving Mishti was not always easy though. Maha and Kailash sheltered Mishti the way they never did with Ahana. They never scolded her for wearing what she wanted, or eating what she liked.

The instructions were exclusively for Ahana. Sometimes she even tried projecting her anger on Mishti, but that was not her. Her guilt would make her go back to her sister and pled for forgiveness.

Sometimes while thinking about the time she spent with Maa, Ahana wondered how Maa was able to maintain her kind and loving attitude in the environment they stayed in. This question kept Ahana from losing hope in the most difficult times. *If Maa could love me despite everything she faced, I can spread love too.*

She channelised this energy towards Mishti. She encouraged her sister to do creative activities, to share the happenings of the day. They went out sometimes, just the two of them, for a quick snack or a walk. These moments were precious, to both of them.

Sharing this love with Mishti, made Ahana realise the power of giving. Slowly she started opening up again. She had started by helping her friends with school work and has continued the legacy throughout her college life. Even during peak exam stress, she would answer calls from her friends to resolve their doubts.

One late evening, during her semester end exam prep, she was struggling to complete her revision. Her legs ached from being seated for too long. Her eyes hurt and her head pounded as she went on and on with the lessons. Despite all that she attended a call, and helped her friend Sanjana with an entire chapter, which she had already completed.

After completing her explanation, she let out a long sigh, "That's it! Hope that helped you." She smiled and looked at her friend's face on the screen. Sanjana looked back at her, "Oh yes! That would do. Okay, bye." "Uh yeah, by the...," Ahana was cut off. The call ended abruptly. *Your welcome, I guess? Sigh.* Ahana sat there looking at her phone breathing deeply for a minute, contemplating, as her eyes stared into the void.

Giving was fun in the beginning, but soon she got frustrated for not being on the receiving end yet that didn't stop her. She knew there will be a day when someone in need will cherish her for her nature and appreciate her help.

It took two more years for Ahana before she successfully built that bond with Shalini. With trial and error, Ahana understood that some people would talk to her only because they need something. Ahana helped them anyways, she just stopped expecting anything in return. She learnt the importance of having people like Shalini in her life. She worked on creating more bonds like that.

Ahana continues to learn. She learns each day about how much is too much, that giving shouldn't exhaust one. She continues to help, but draws a line so people don't take advantage of her. She is also working on achieving her dreams. She set of by exploring various things, but it was writing in which she found the kick she was looking for.

I am going to be a published author one day.

This is a dream she shared with very few, the few she knew would encourage her to strive hard to make it.

And she finally set out to write her first story and it began thus,

Dreams cannot die even if you do. That's why we ought to achieve our dreams and become who we want to be. Your strength

and goodness will make you get through it in life. You deserve to be loved for who you are.

She published her book in her final year of graduation. What a thrill it was for her. And she dedicated her book to all those who are struggling and fighting for their dreams.

Call for Submissions

Theme: My Greatest Joy

There are many things that make us happy, but very few that give us true joy. The inner bliss that makes us excited with a sense of calmness to it.

We invite you to submit your stories and tell us about the one thing or person that gave you that joy, or helped you find it within.

Submission Guidelines:

Please submit your stories as an editable Word document.

There is no age limit to be an author.

Language: English

Word Limit: 2000- 5000 words

Font: Times New Roman, 12

Spacing: 1.5

Deadline: 31ˢᵗ July 2024

Manuscripts will be reviewed within a month from the deadline of submission (by August 31st)

Authors can expect to hear from us with one of the following responses: Accepted, Revision Required, Submission Declined.

There is **no submission or publication charges.**

We currently cannot offer payments for the stories published. However, along with the recognition as a published author; as our generous thanks to the authors of the selected stories, we would be offering a small reward in the form of a gift.

Looking forward to hearing from you!

For submissions or any queries regarding submissions, feel free to send us an email: sv.shortfiction@gmail.com